Coming Up

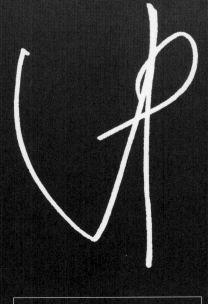

POLYGRAM MUSIC PUBLISHING LIMITED

psycho we'll dank office in A
in the petrol furniture black
fumes... chair...

SAt there

Arse of

the litter

MA

the Natio

bARKing

notation & tablature explained   4

Tablature & Instructions Explained

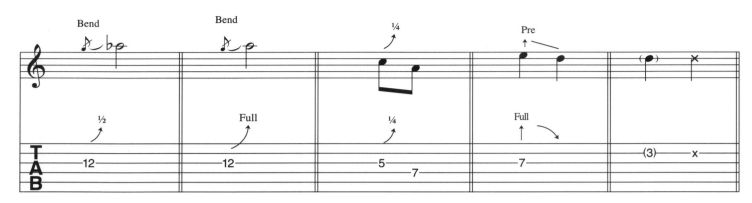

HALF TONE BEND

Play the note G then bend the string so that the pitch rises by a half tone (semi-tone).

FULL TONE BEND

DECORATIVE BEND

PRE-BEND

Bend the string as indicated, strike the string and release.

GHOST NOTES

The first note is half sounded. The second is totally muted to produce a percussive effect.

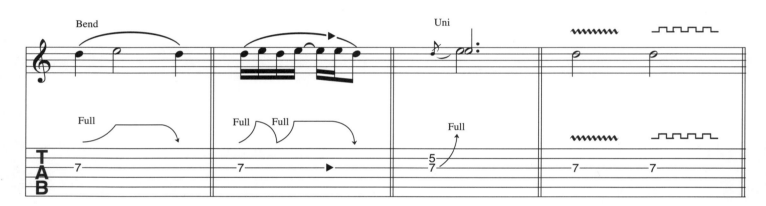

BEND & RELEASE

Strike the string, bend it as indicated, then release the bend whilst it is still sounding.

BEND & RESTRIKE

Strike the string, bend or gliss as indicated, then restrike the string where the symbol occurs.

UNISON BEND

Strike both strings simultaneously then immediately bend the lower string as indicated.

VIBRATO

The first note is played with finger vibrato, the second with tremolo arm vibrato.

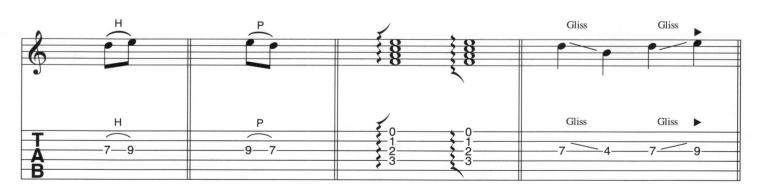

HAMMER-ON

Hammer a finger down on the next note without striking the string again.

PULL-OFF

Pull your finger off the string with a plucking motion to sound the next note without striking the string again.

RAKE-UP/DOWN

Strum the notes upwards or downwards in the manner of an arpeggio.

GLISSANDO

Strike the note, then slide the finger up or down the fretboard as indicated. Restrike the string where the symbol occurs.

trash

Words & Music by Brett Anderson & Richard Oakes

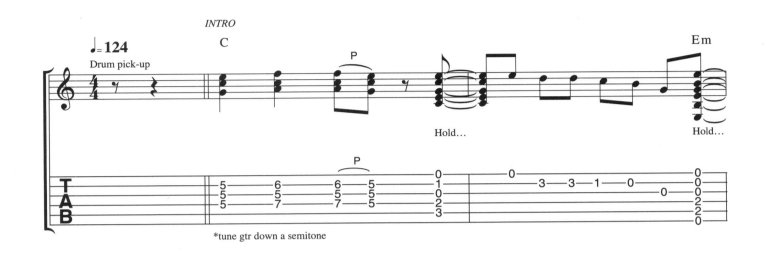

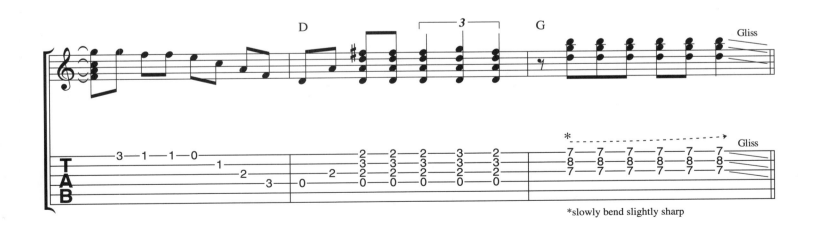

VERSE

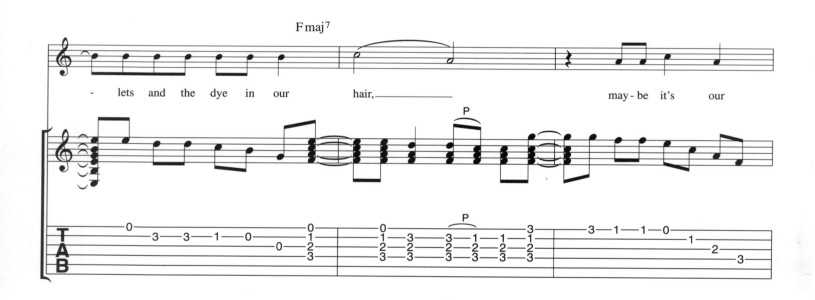

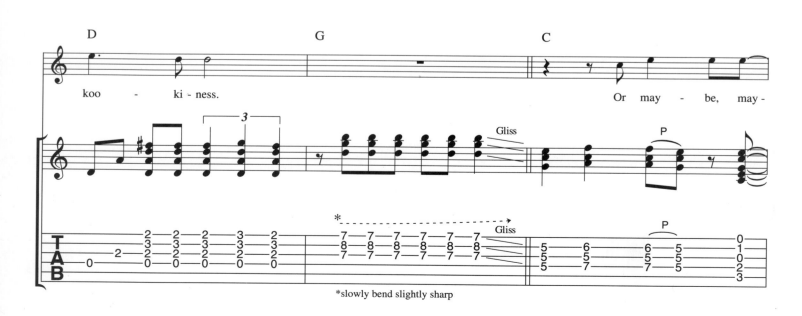

*slowly bend slightly sharp

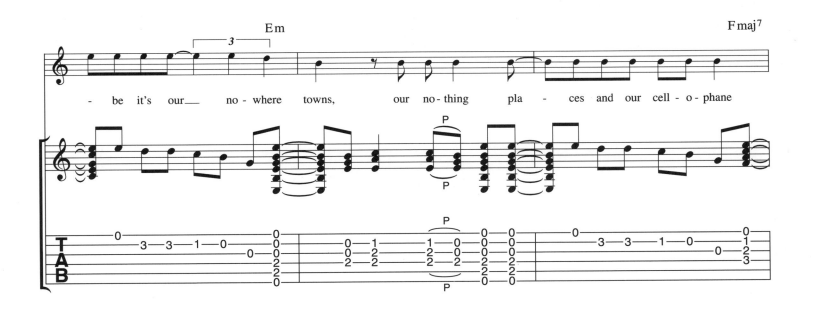

- be it's our___ no - where towns, our no - thing pla - ces and our cell - o - phane

sounds,___ may - be it's our loose - ness.___

CHORUS

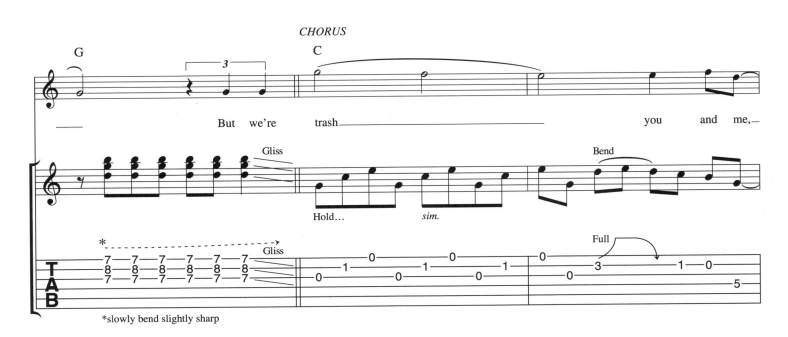

But we're trash___ you and me,___

Hold... *sim.*

*slowly bend slightly sharp

we're the lit - ter on the breeze,— we're the

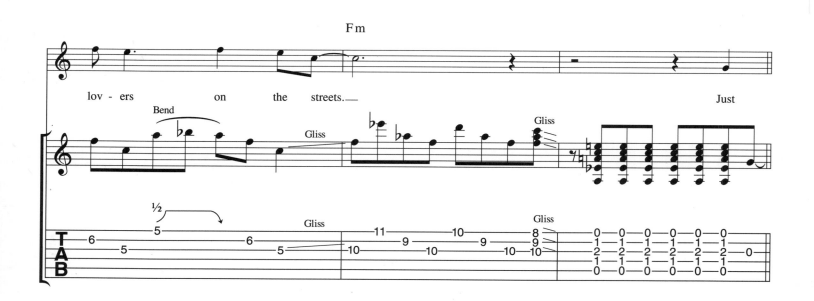

lov - ers on the streets.— Just

trash————————————— me and you,— it's in

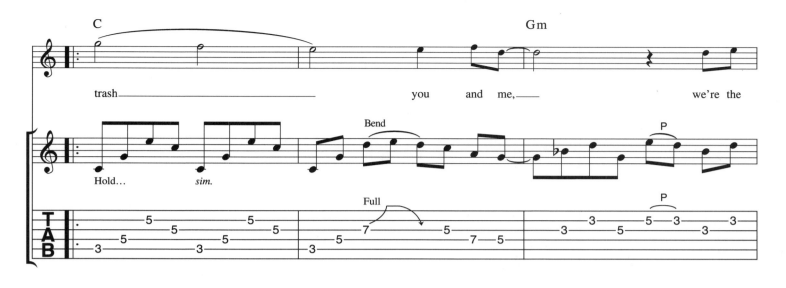

trash _____ you and me, _____ we're the

Hold… sim.

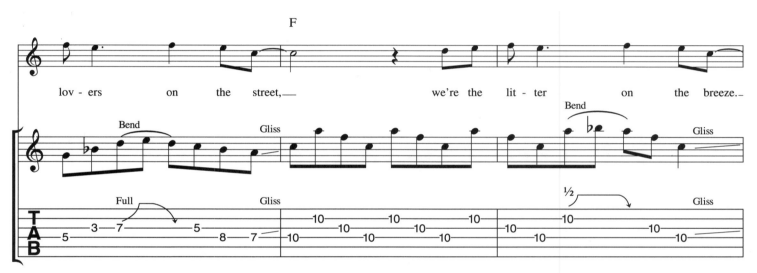

lov-ers on the street, _____ we're the lit-ter on the breeze.__

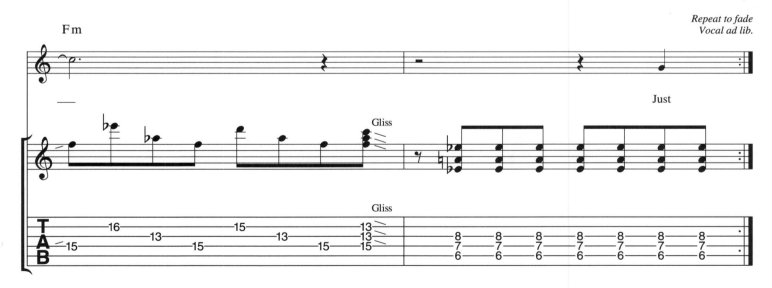

Repeat to fade
Vocal ad lib.

Just

Verse 2:
Or maybe, maybe it's the things we say
The words we've heard and the music we play
Maybe it's our cheapness
Or maybe, maybe it's the times we've had
The lazy days and the crazes and the fads
Maybe it's our sweetness.

filmstar

Words & Music by Brett Anderson & Richard Oakes

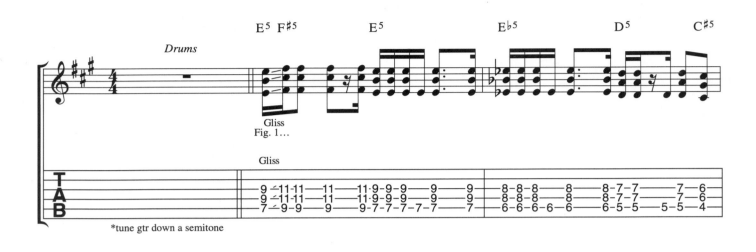

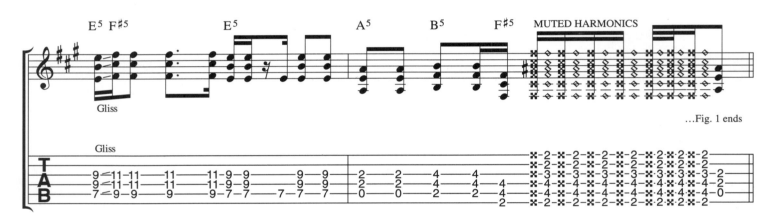

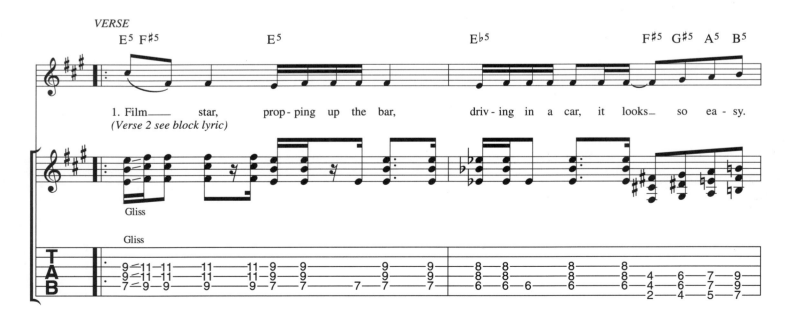

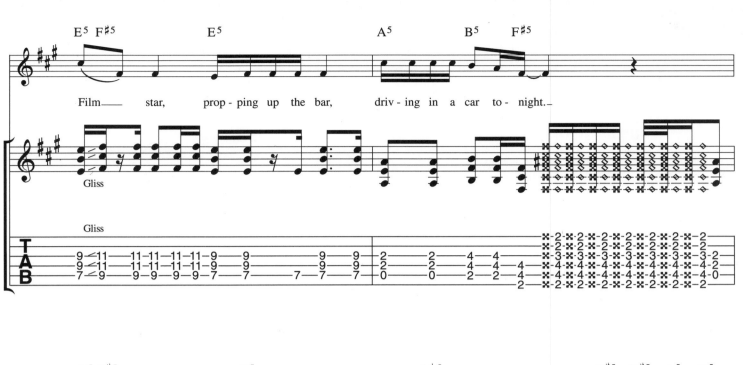

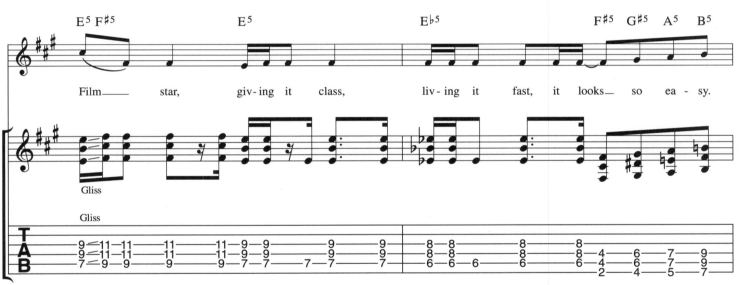

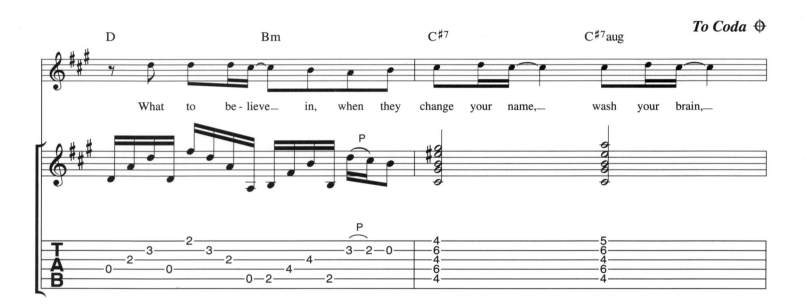

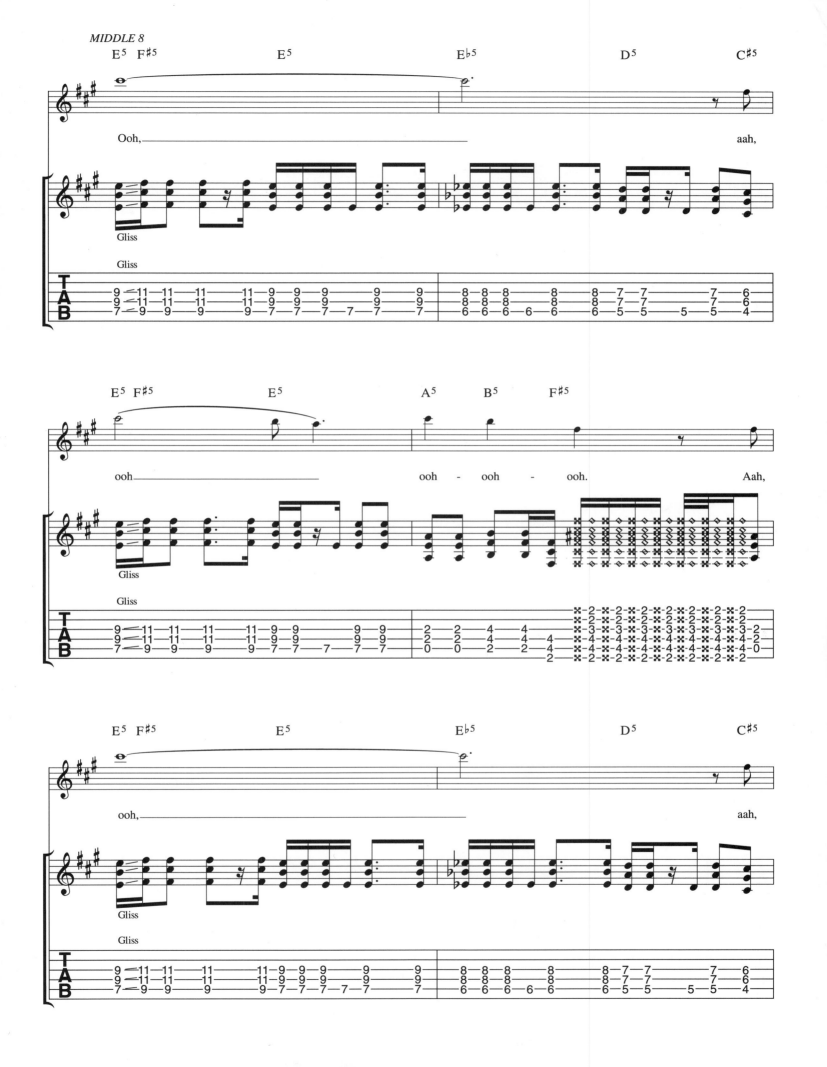

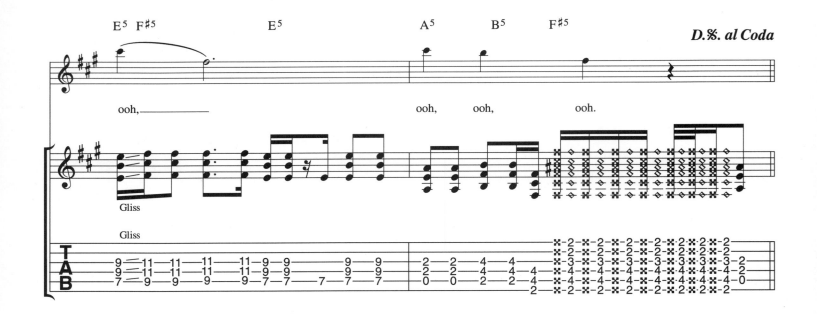

D.%. al Coda

ooh,_____ ooh, ooh, ooh.

✛ *Coda*

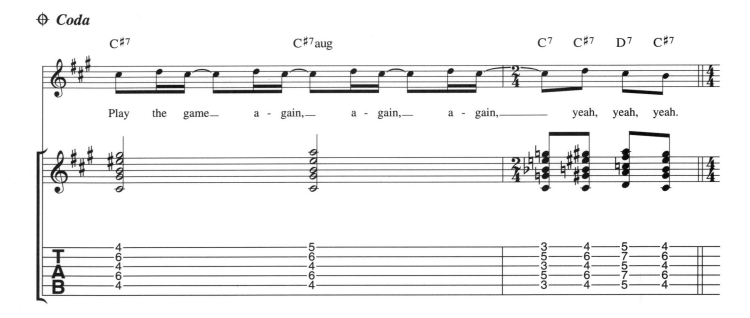

Play the game— a - gain,— a - gain,— a - gain,_____ yeah, yeah, yeah.

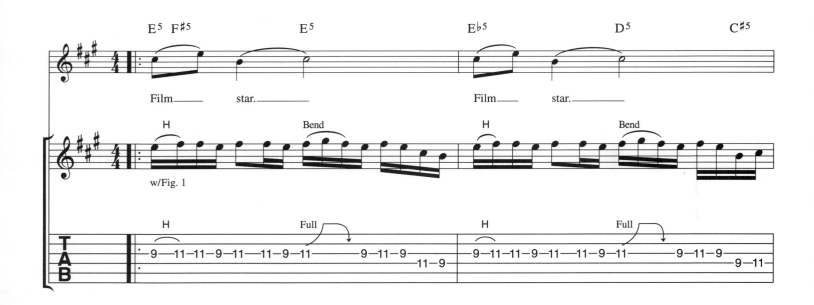

Film___ star._____ Film___ star._____

w/Fig. 1

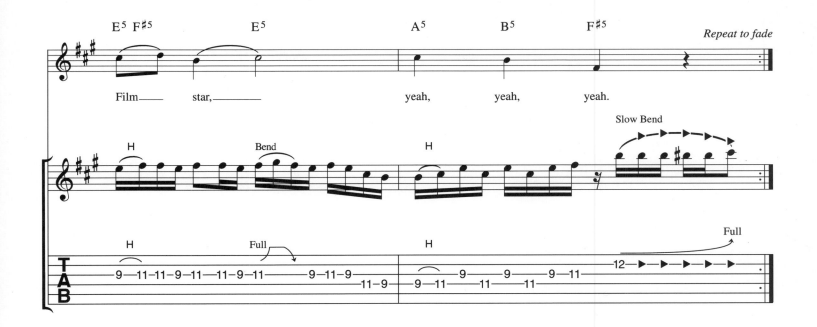

Verse 2:
Filmstar, elegance, a terylene shirt, it looks so easy
Filmstar, an elegant sir in a terylene shirt tonight
Filmstar, propping up the bar, driving in a car, it looks so easy
Filmstar, propping up the bar, driving in a car tonight.

lazy

Words & Music by Brett Anderson

*tune gtr down a semitone

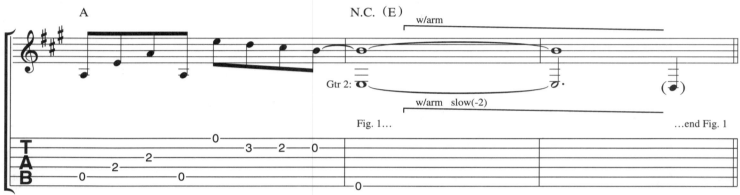

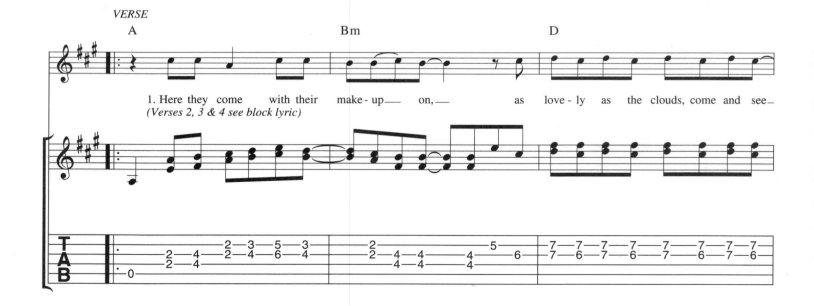

1. Here they come with their make-up on, — as love-ly as the clouds, come and see—
(Verses 2, 3 & 4 see block lyric)

CHORUS

But you and me, all we want to be_____ is la - zy._____

Let ring...

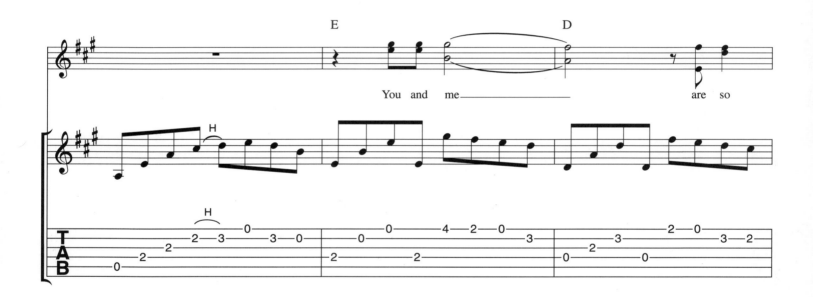

You and me_____ are so

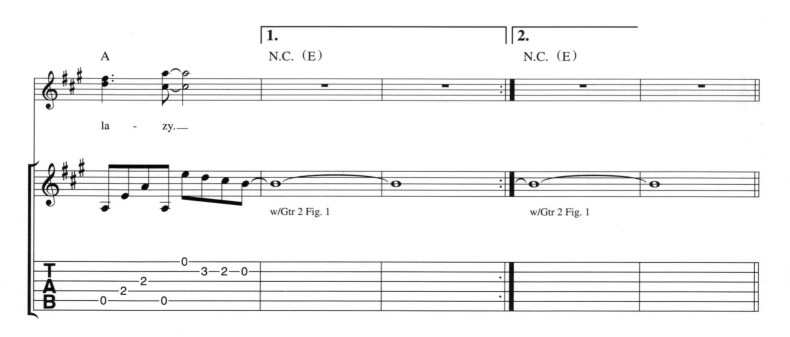

la - zy._____

w/Gtr 2 Fig. 1   w/Gtr 2 Fig. 1

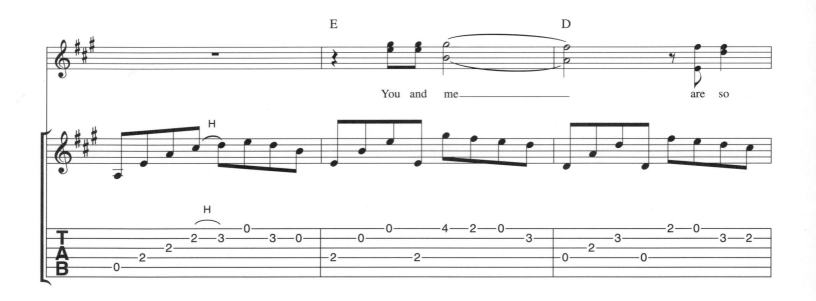

You and me _____ are so

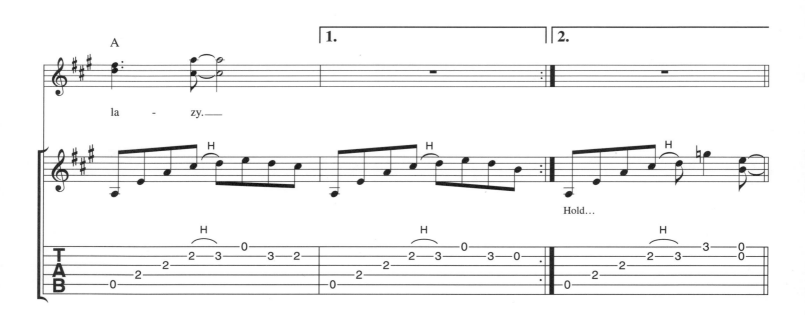

1.

2.

la - zy. _____

Hold...

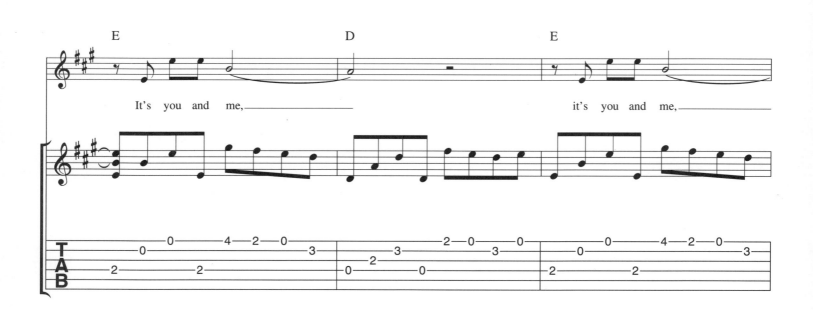

It's you and me, _____ it's you and me, _____

it's you and me.

Verse 2:
Barking mad kids, lonely dads
Who drug it up to give it some meaning
From the raves to the council estates
They're reminding us there's things to be done.

Verse 3:
Here they come, gone 7 a.m
Getting satellite and Sky, getting cable
Bills and Bens and their mums and their friends
Who just really, really want to be loved.

Verse 4:
Uncle Teds and their legendary vests
Helping out around the disabled
From the flats and the maisonettes
They're reminding us there's things to be done.

we're the litter

BARKing

Arse ot
the Nati

FLAT on
her back

MAybe we're
just kids

by the sea

Words & Music by Brett Anderson

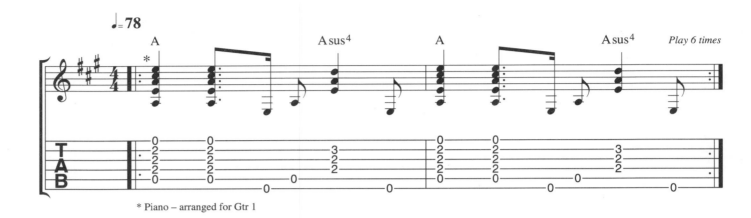

* Piano – arranged for Gtr 1

VERSE

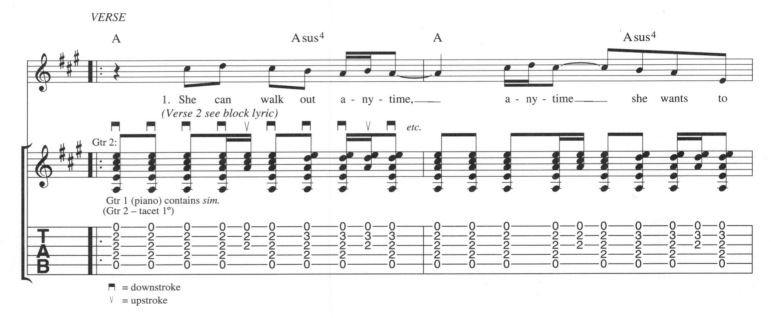

1. She can walk out a - ny - time,___ a - ny - time___ she wants to
(Verse 2 see block lyric)

Gtr 2:

etc.

Gtr 1 (piano) contains *sim.*
(Gtr 2 – tacet 1°)

⊓ = downstroke
V = upstroke

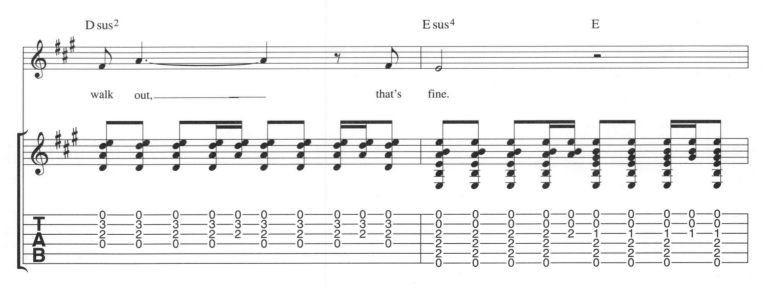

walk out,___ that's fine.

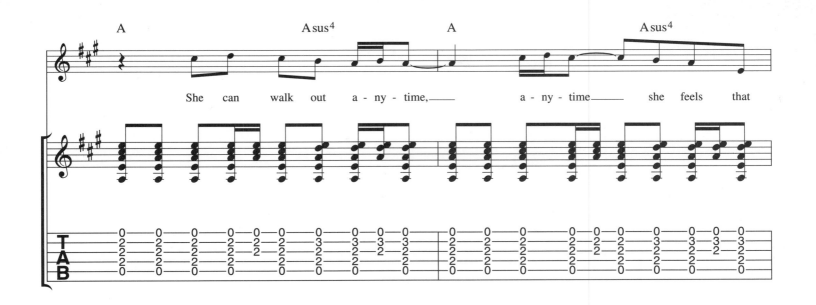

She can walk out a-ny-time,_____ a-ny-time_____ she feels that

life has passed her by.

Gtr 3: – electric (with overdrive)
Gtr 2 continues *sim.*

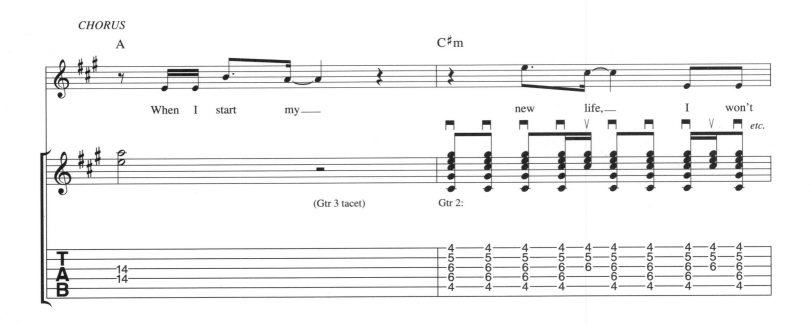

CHORUS

When I start my____ new life,____ I won't *etc.*

(Gtr 3 tacet)   Gtr 2:

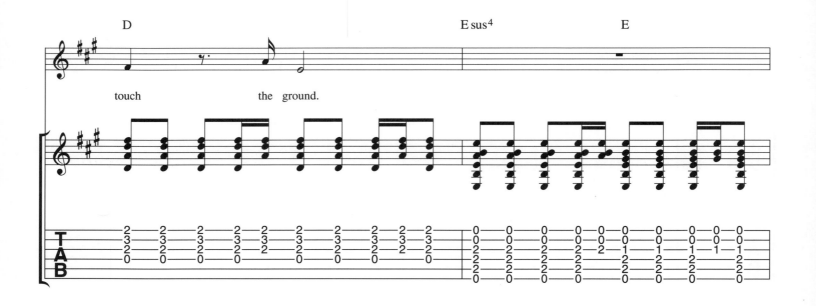

touch   the ground.

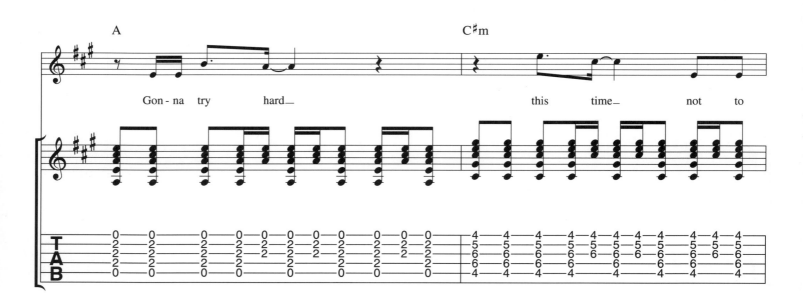

Gon - na try hard—   this   time—   not   to

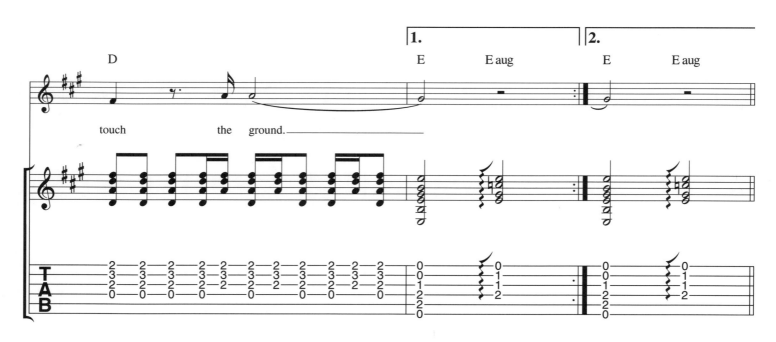

touch   the ground.————

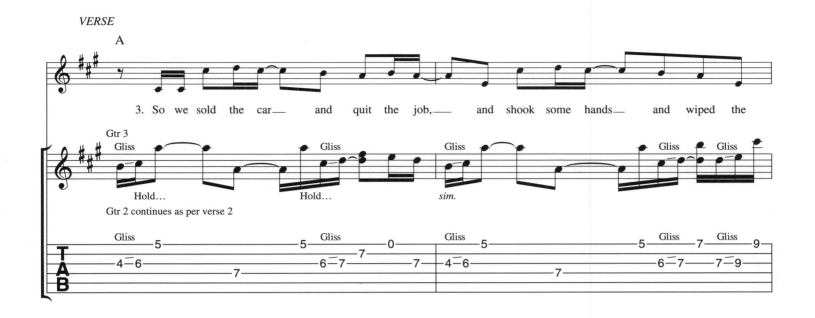

3. So we sold the car—— and quit the job,—— and shook some hands—— and wiped the

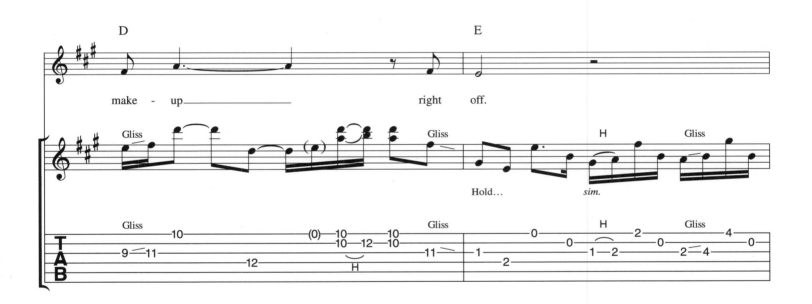

make - up—————————— right off.

We said our good - byes to the bank, left Sev - en Sis - ters for a

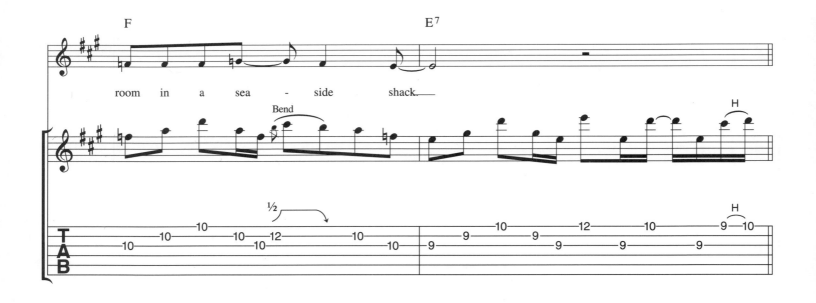

room   in   a   sea - side   shack.__

CHORUS

When I   start   my__   new life,__   I won't   touch   the ground.

Gon - na   try   hard__   this   time__   not to

Verse 2:
He can walk out anytime, anytime he wants to walk out, that's fine
He can walk out anytime, cross the sand into the sea, into the brine.

she

Words & Music by Brett Anderson & Richard Oakes

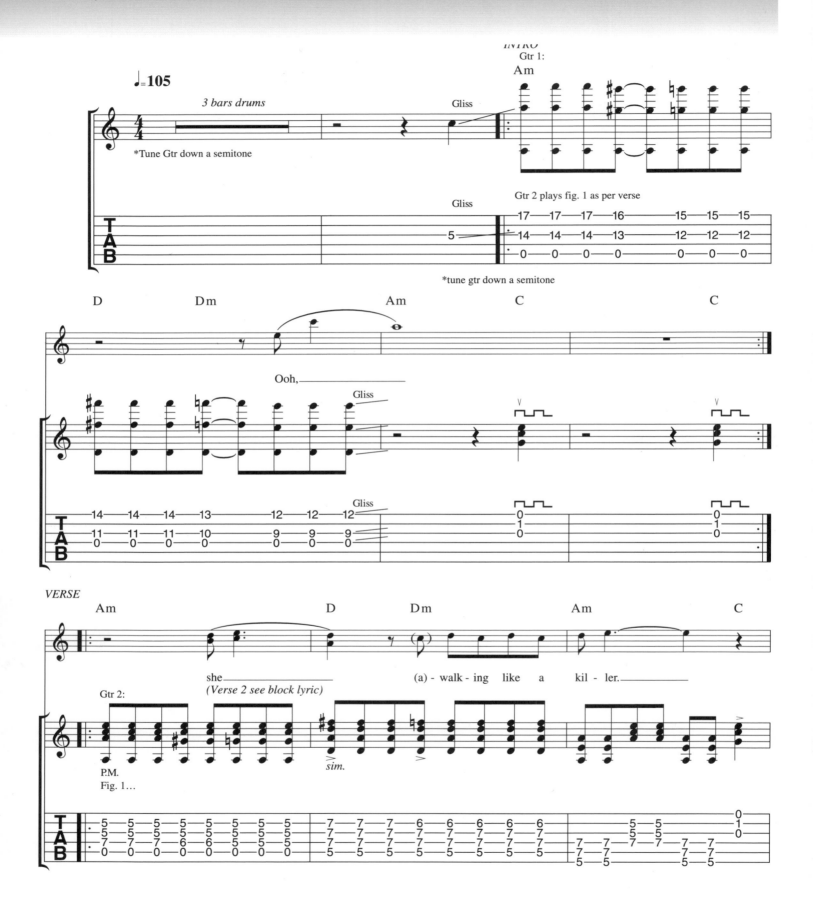

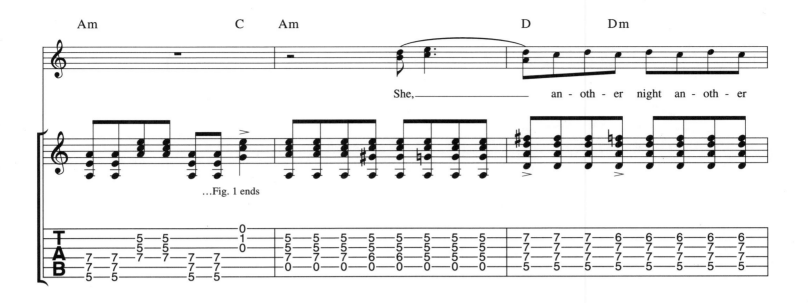

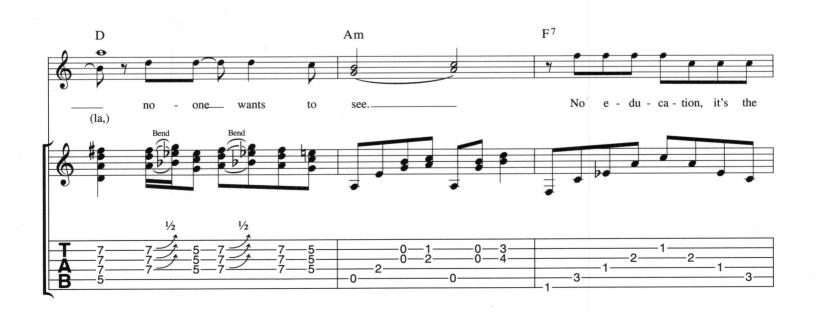

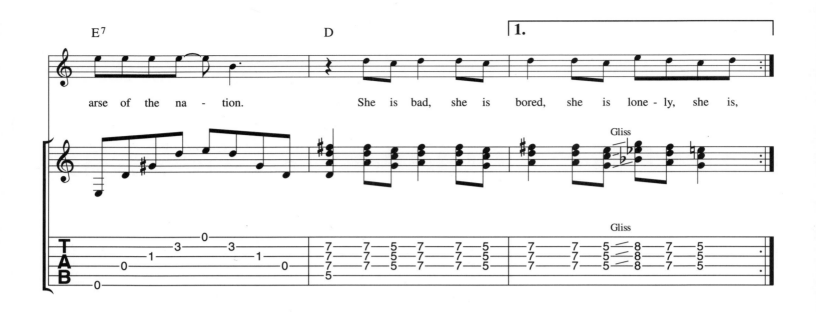

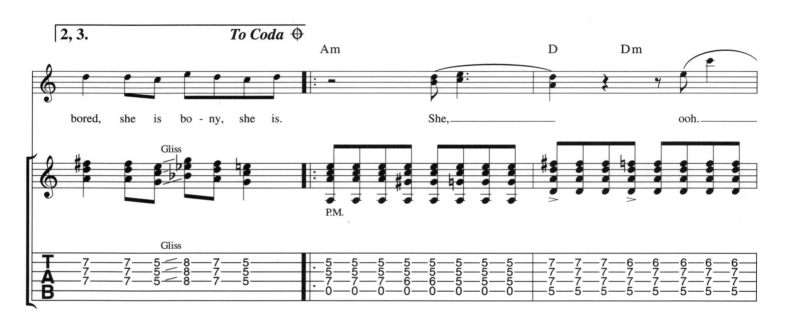

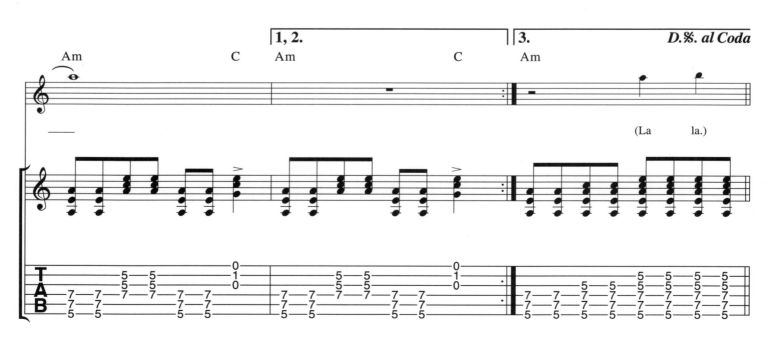

Coda

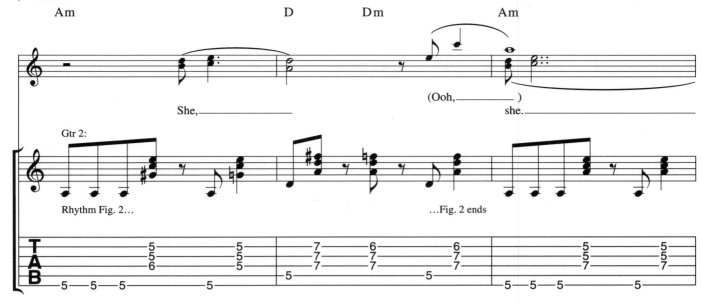

She,_____

(Ooh,_____)   she._____

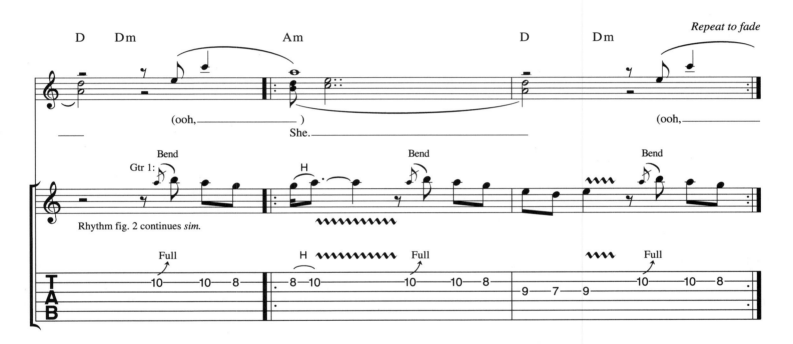

(ooh,_____)   (ooh,_____)

She._____

Verse 2:
She, sh-shaking up the karma
She, "injecting marijuana."

Chorus on (%):
Nowhere faces, nowhere places
No one wants to be
No stimulation in this privatisation
She is bad, she is bored, she is bony, she is she.

beautiful ones

Words & Music by Brett Anderson & Richard Oakes

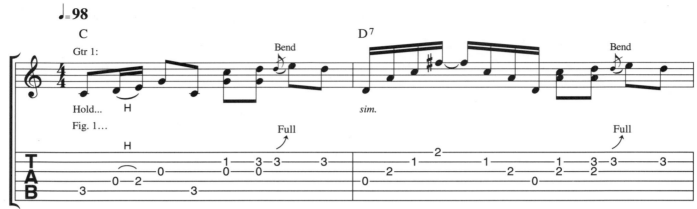

*tune gtr down one semitone

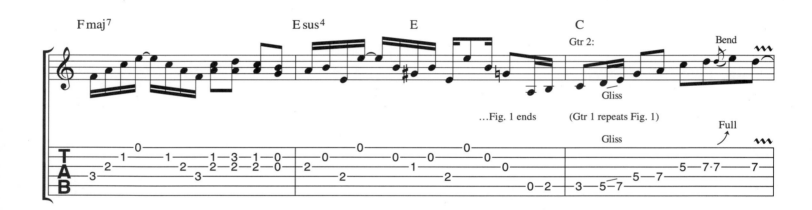

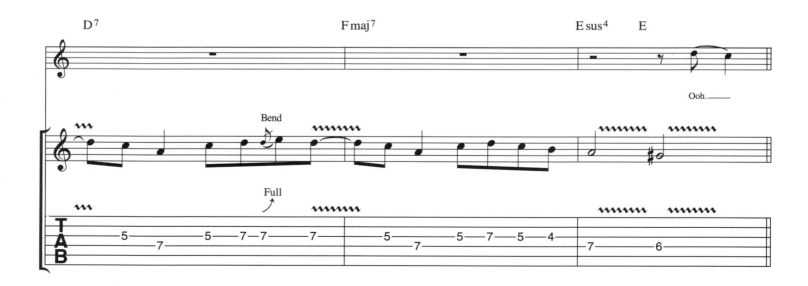

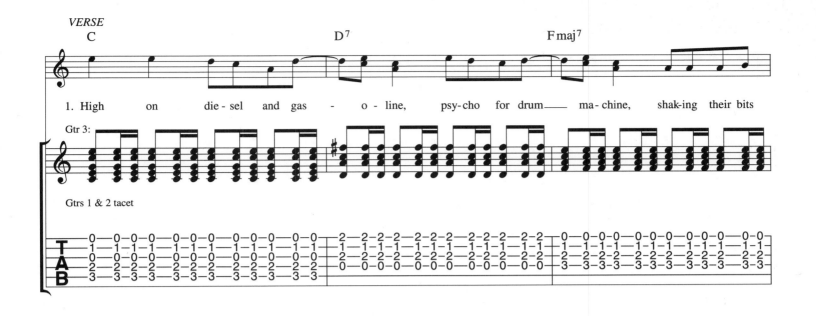

VERSE

1. High on die-sel and gas-o-line, psy-cho for drum machine, shak-ing their bits

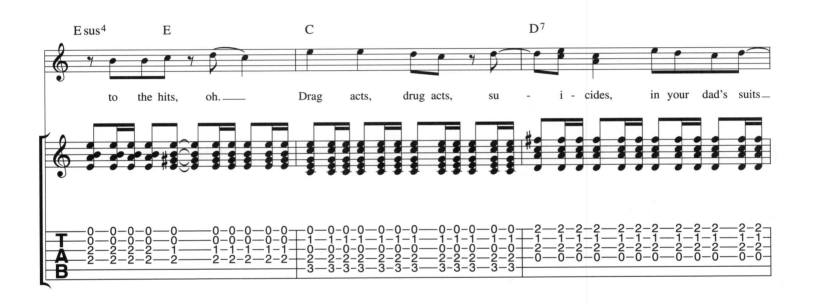

to the hits, oh. Drag acts, drug acts, su-i-cides, in your dad's suits

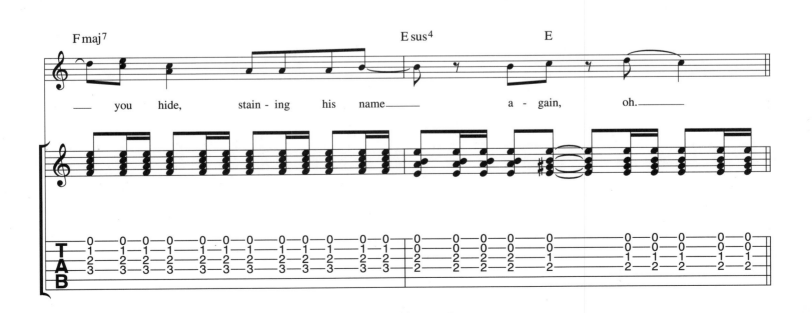

you hide, stain-ing his name a-gain, oh.

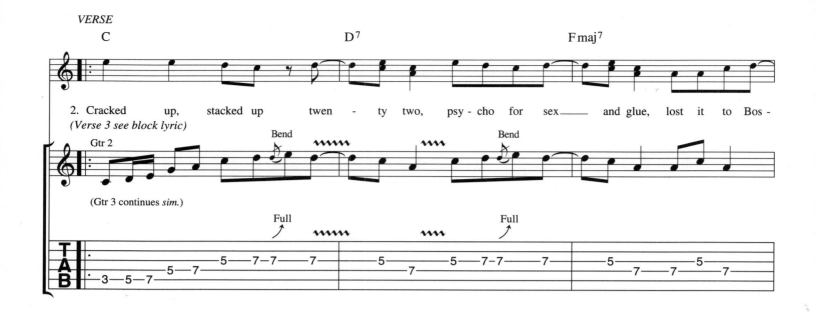

2. Cracked up, stacked up twen - ty two, psy - cho for sex___ and glue, lost it to Bos -
(Verse 3 see block lyric)

- tik, yeah. Oh,___ shaved heads, rave heads, on___ the pill, got too much time___

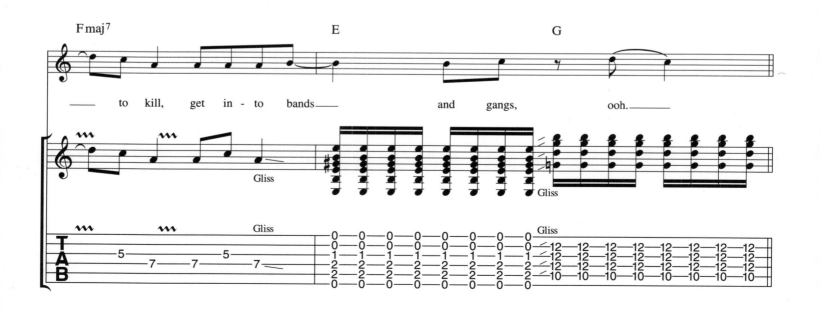

___ to kill, get in - to bands___ and gangs, ooh.___

CHORUS

Here they come,— the beau-ti-ful ones,— the beau-ti-ful ones,—

la la la la.— Here they come,— the beau-ti ful ones,— the

1.

beau-ti-ful ones,— la la la la— la. La la

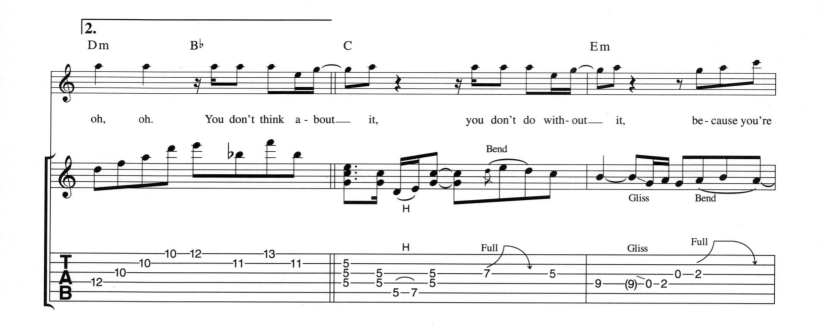

oh, oh. You don't think a-bout— it, you don't do with-out— it, be-cause you're

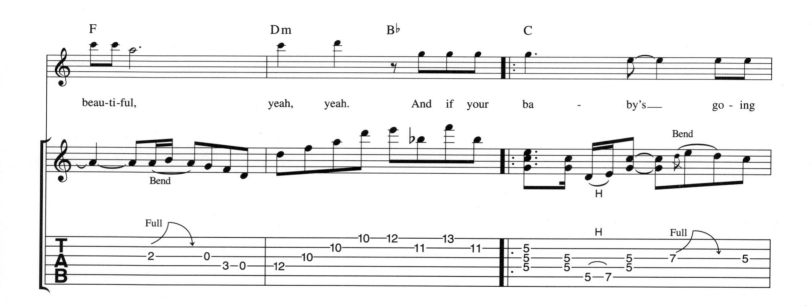

beau-ti-ful, yeah, yeah. And if your ba - by's— go - ing

cra - zy,— that's how you made— me,— la la. And if your

40

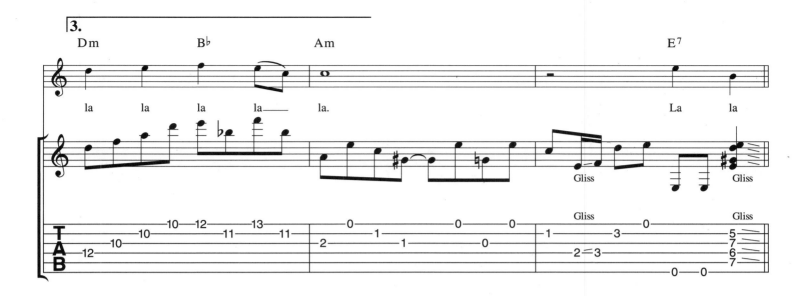

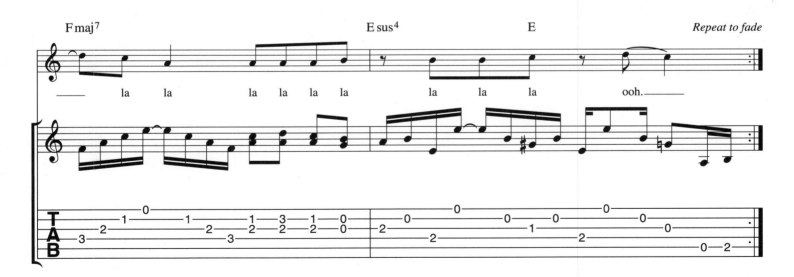

Verse 3:
Loved up, doved up, hung around, stoned in a lonely town
Shaking their meat to the beat
High on diesel and gasoline, psycho for drum machine
Shaking their bits to the hits, oh.

echo we'll dunk office in A
in the petrol furniture black
chair ...
Sat there

a the ple
fumes ..

starcrazy

Words & Music by Brett Anderson & Neil Codling

lec-tric-shock - bog-brush hair,—   flat on her back— in the eight-

1.

- ies,   in the nine - ties go-ing no - where.

2, 3.

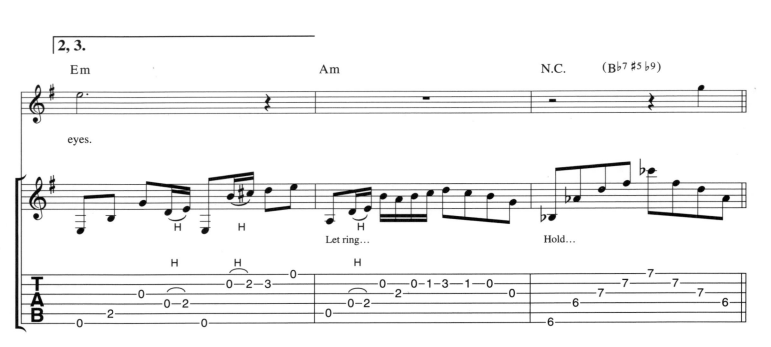

eyes.

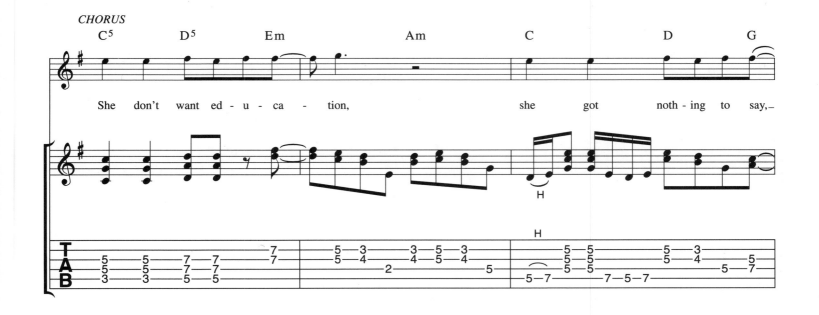

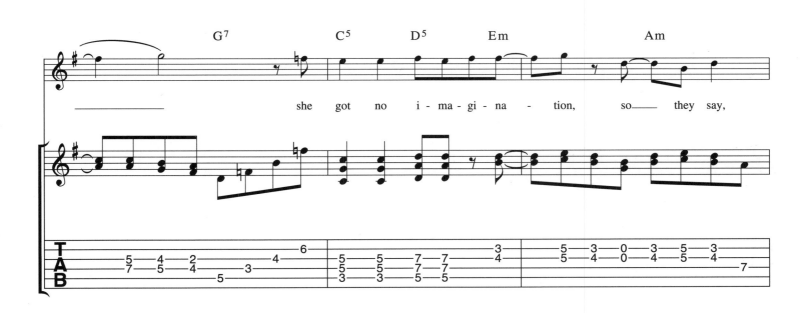

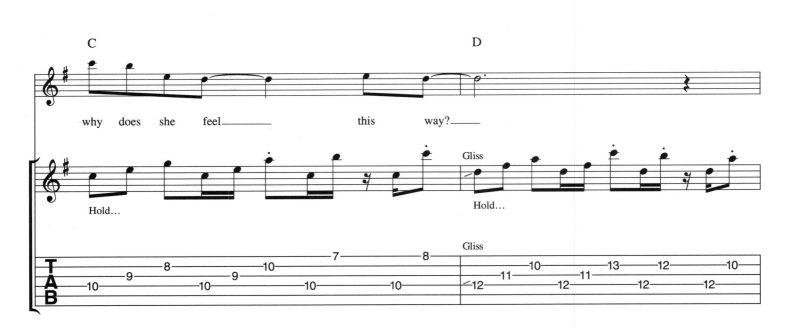

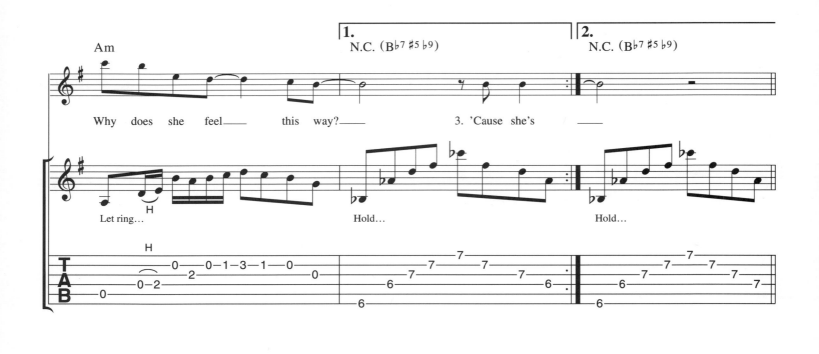

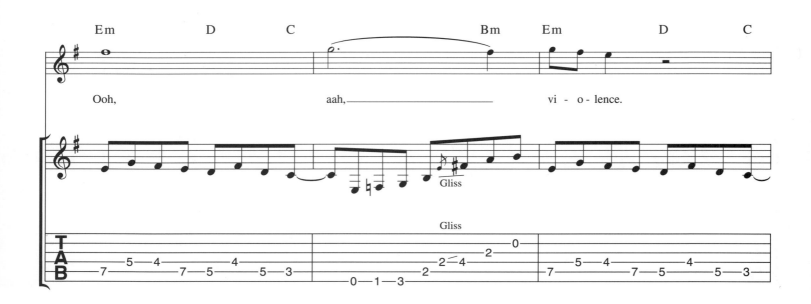

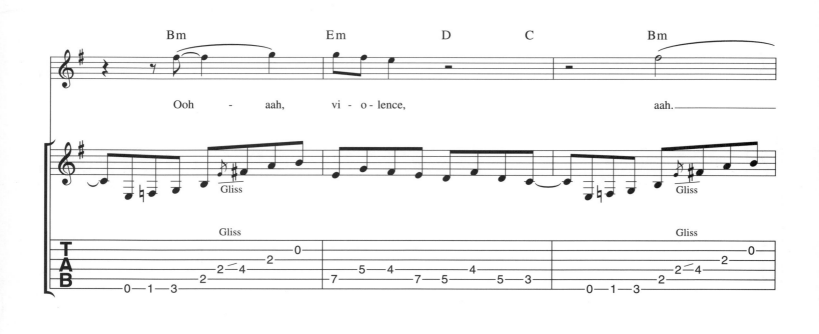

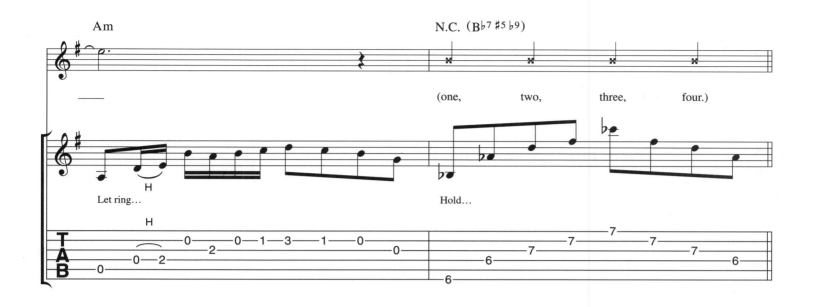

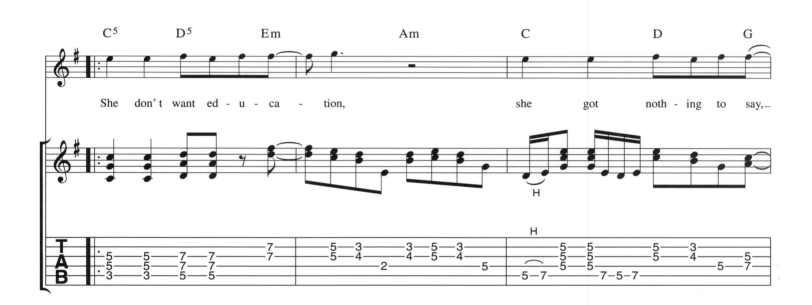

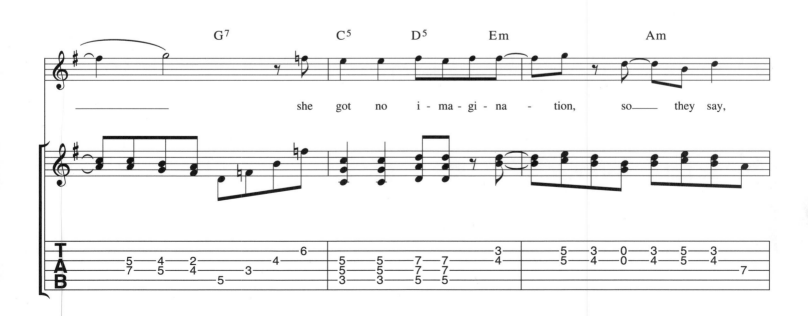

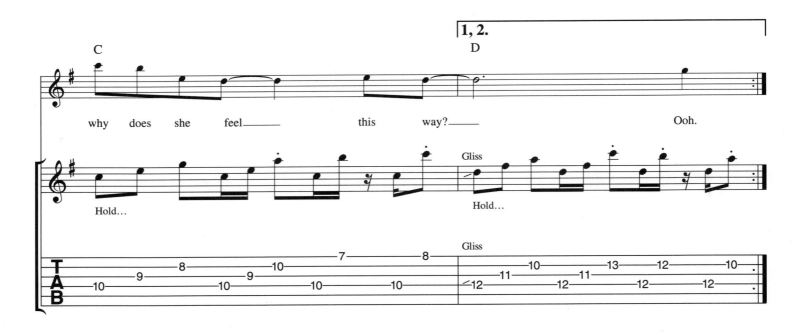

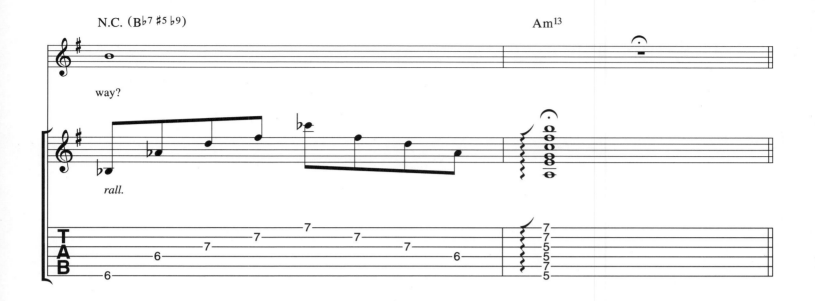

Verse 2:
Star, star crazy, got a kicking transistor inside
A heavy metal stutter that brains me
And an electric love in her eyes.

Verse 3:
'Cause she's star, star crazy
Getting stupid on the streets tonight
And shaking like a mechanical thing
With an electric love in her eyes.

picnic by the motorway

Words & Music by Brett Anderson & Richard Oakes

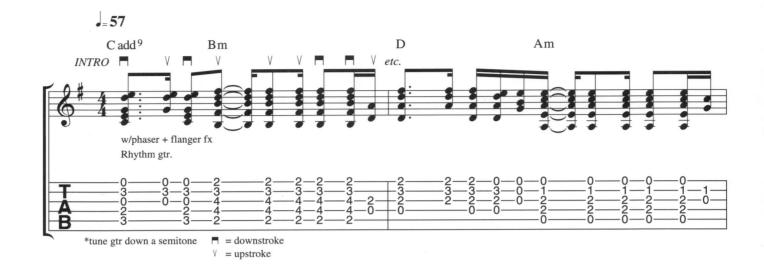

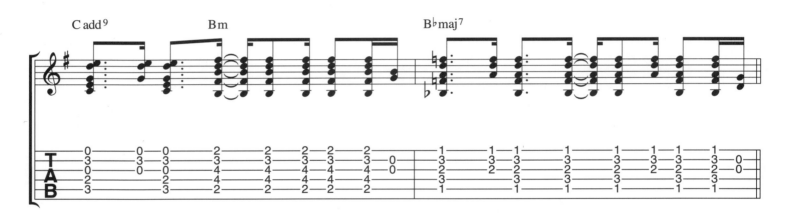

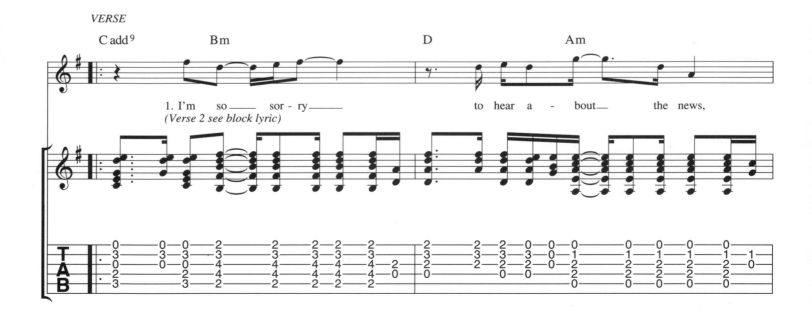

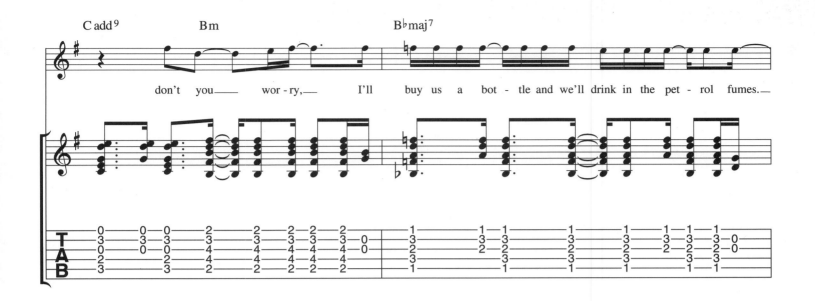

don't you___ wor-ry,___ I'll buy us a bot-tle and we'll drink in the pet-rol fumes.___

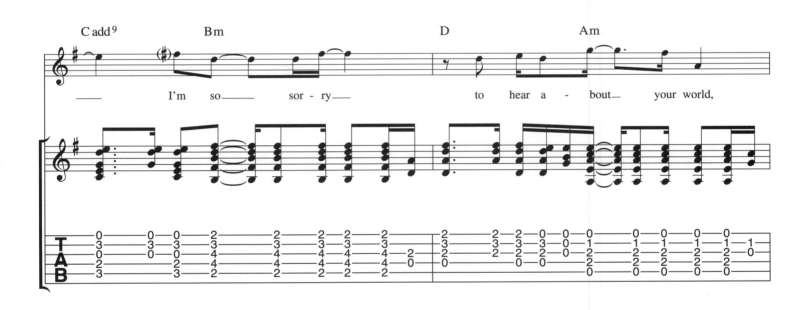

___ I'm so___ sor-ry___ to hear a-bout___ your world,

don't you ___ wor-ry, there's a gap in the fence_down by the na-ture re-serve,___ oh.

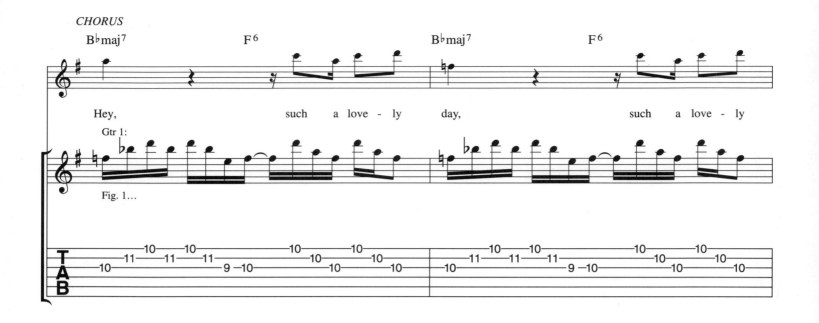

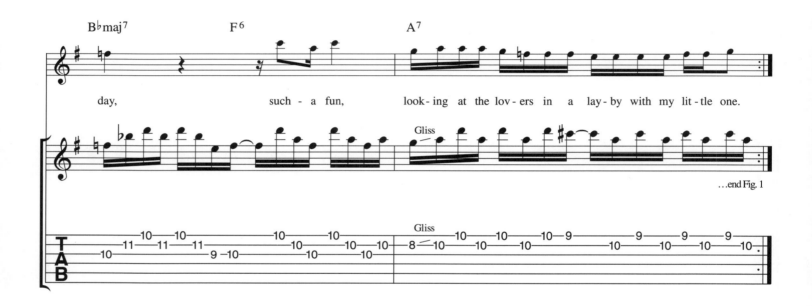

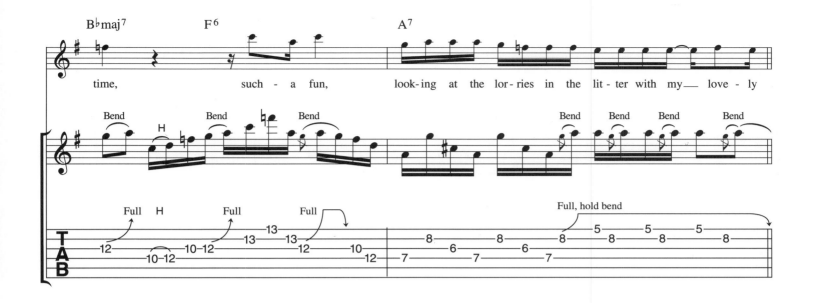

time,   such - a fun,   look-ing at the lor - ries in the lit - ter with my___ love - ly

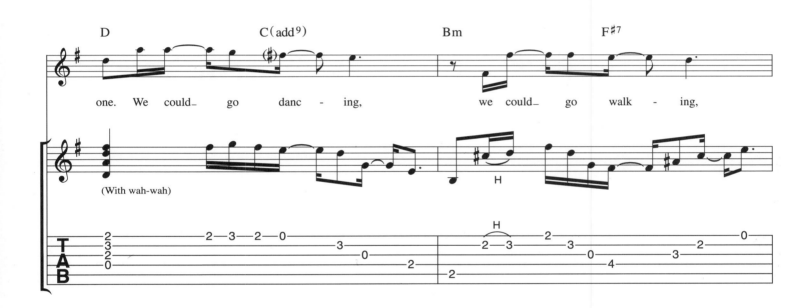

one. We could___ go danc - ing,   we could___ go walk - ing,

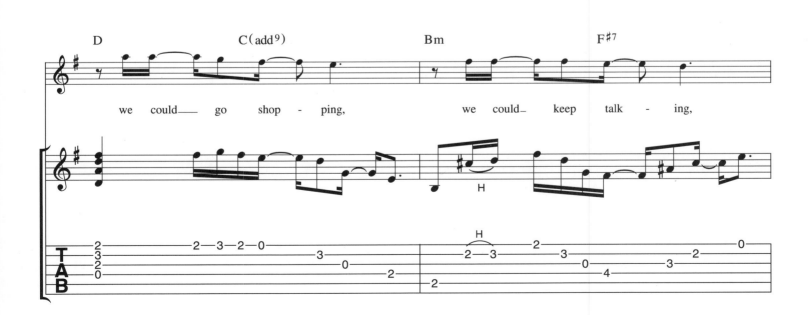

we could___ go shop - ping,   we could___ keep talk - ing,

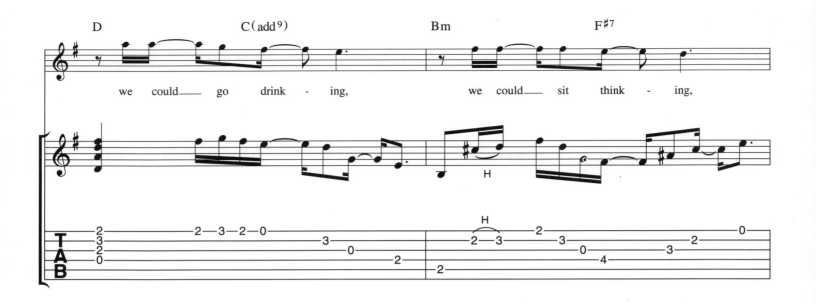

we could— go drink - ing,   we could— sit think - ing,

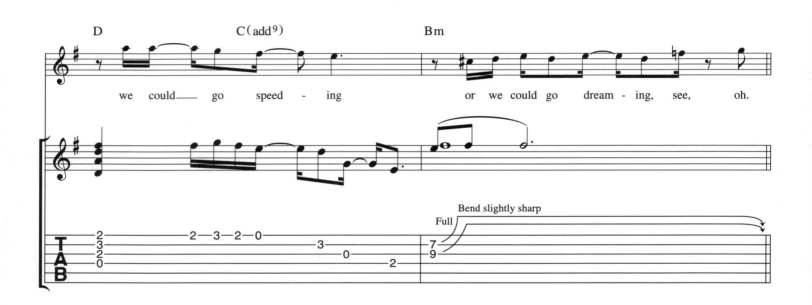

we could— go speed - ing   or we could go dream - ing, see, oh.

Bend slightly sharp
Full

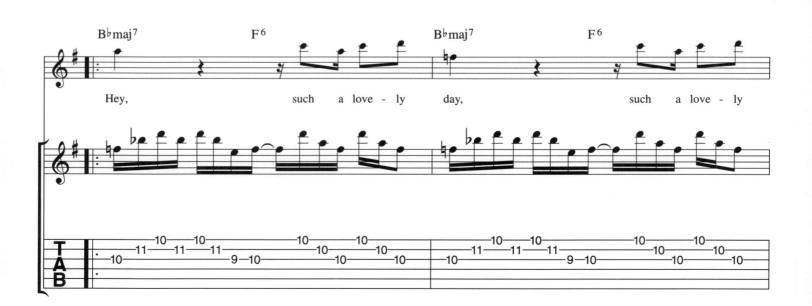

Hey,   such a love - ly day,   such a love - ly

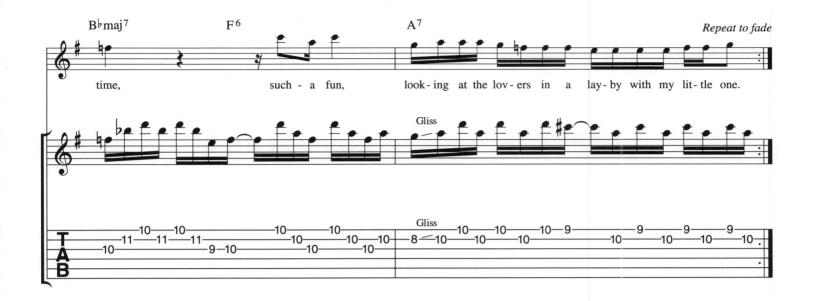

time,   such - a fun,   look - ing at the lov - ers   in   a   lay - by with my lit - tle one.

Verse 2:

I'm so sorry to hear the news today

Don't you worry, there's been a speeding disaster so we'll go to the motorway

I'm so sorry to hear about the scene

Don't you worry, just put on your trainers and get out of it with me.

the chemistry between us

Words & Music by Brett Anderson & Neil Codling

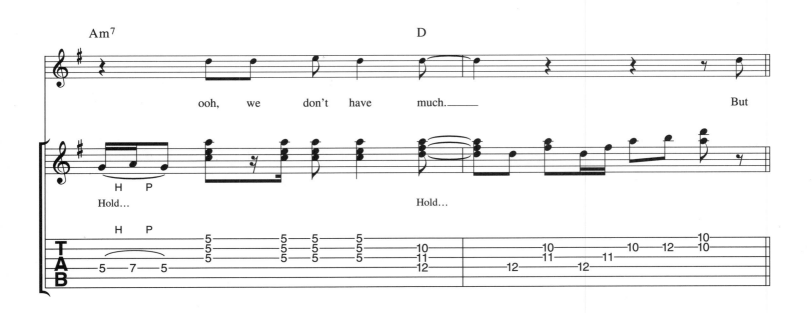

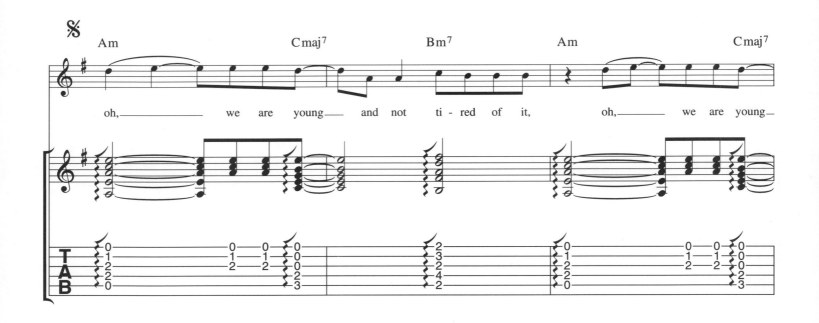

oh, _____ we are young ___ and not ti - red of it, oh, _____ we are young ___

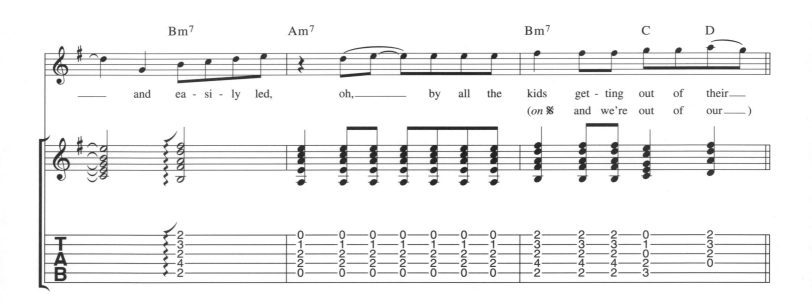

___ and ea - si - ly led, oh, _____ by all the kids get - ting out of their ___
(on % and we're out of our ___)

CHORUS

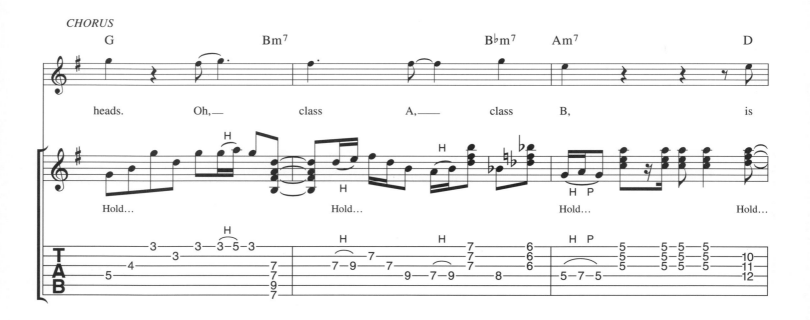

heads. Oh, ___ class A, ___ class B, is

Hold...   Hold...   Hold...   Hold...

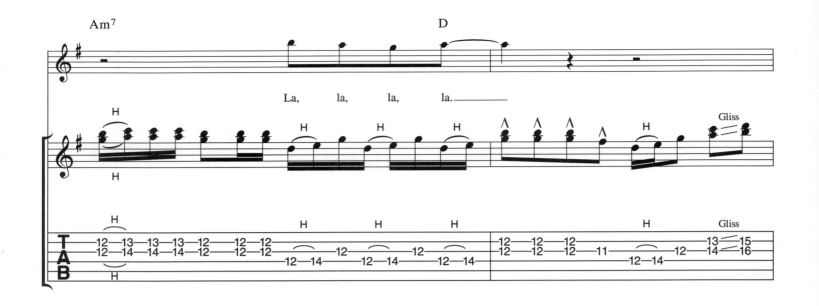

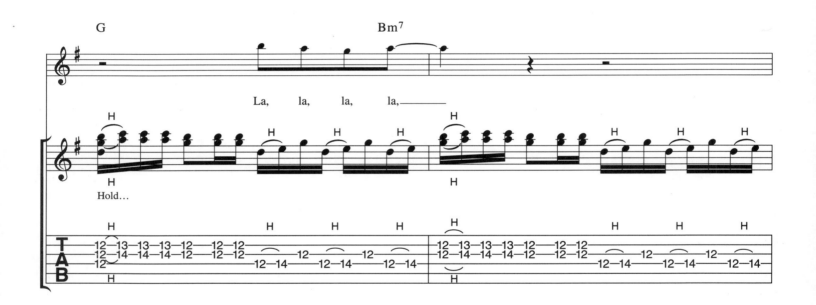

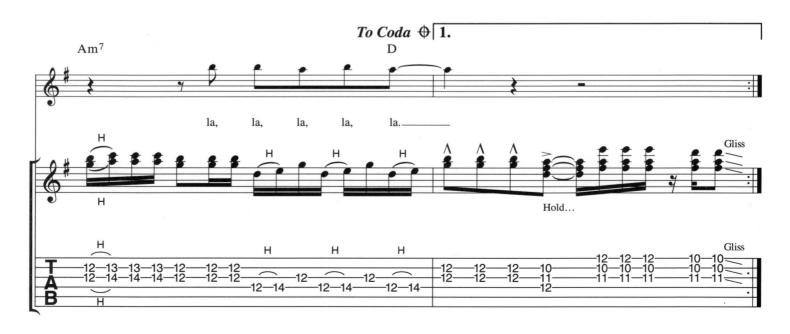

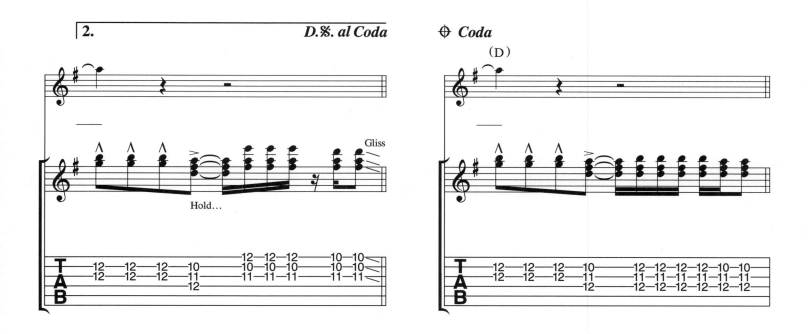

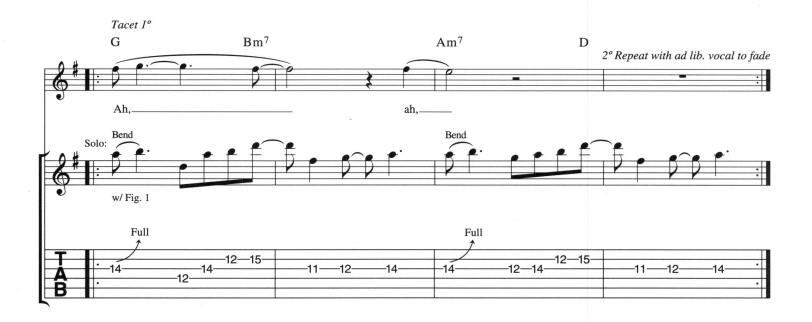

Verse 2:
And maybe we're just Streatham trash
And maybe not
And maybe we're just capital flash
In a stupid love.
But oh, we are young, *etc…*

then we'll dank
'in the petrol
fumes ...

ice

nitre

black

chair ...

saturday night

Words & Music by Brett Anderson & Richard Oakes

*tune gtr down a semitone

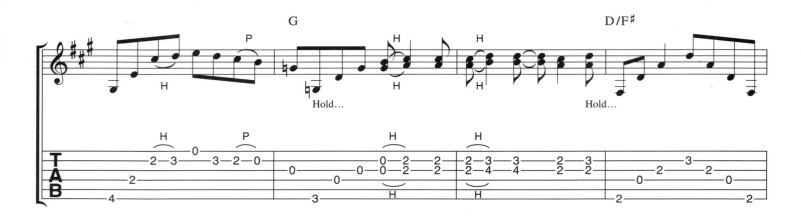

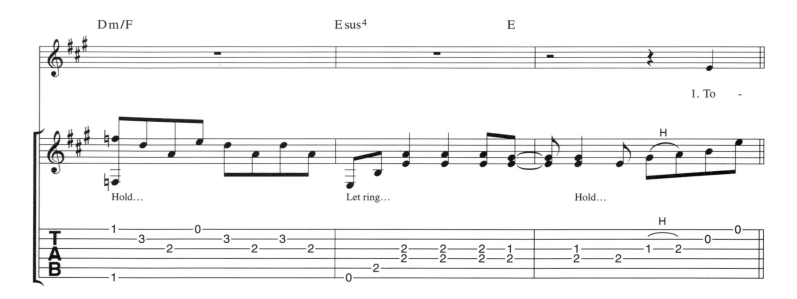

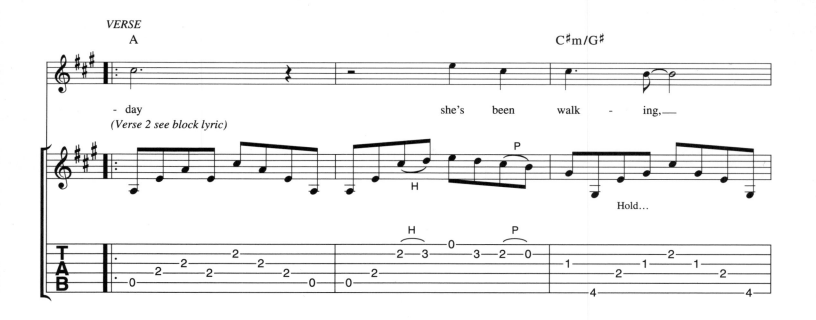

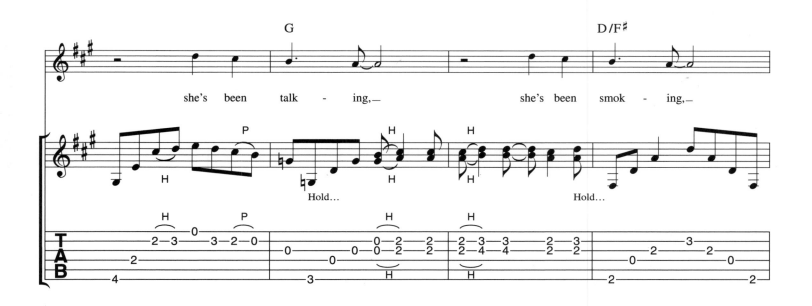

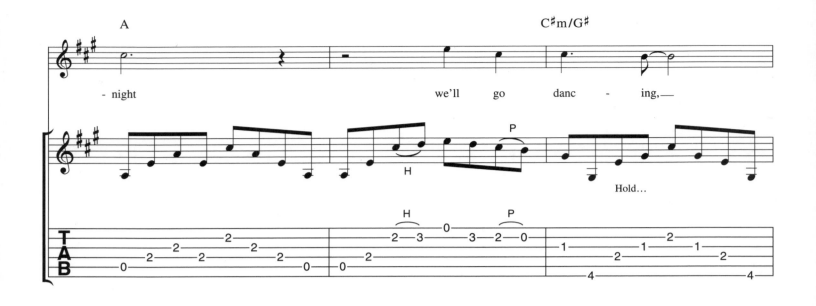

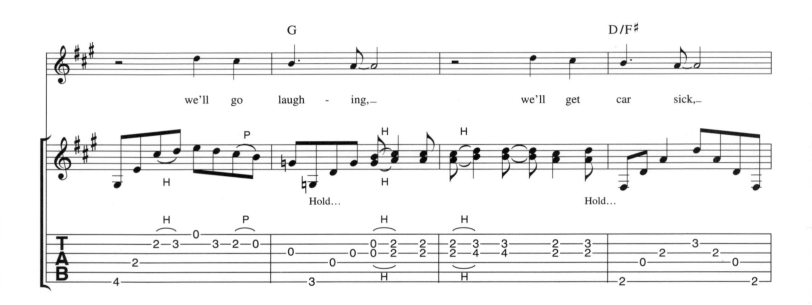

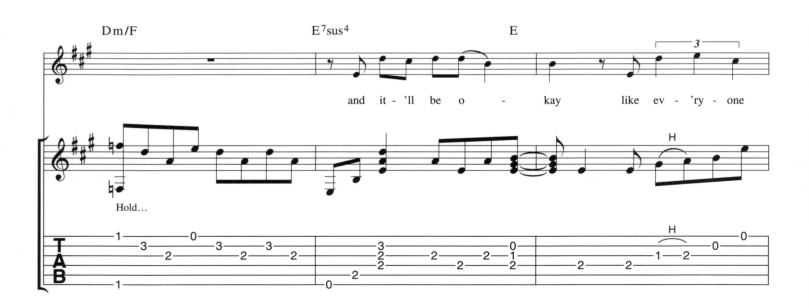

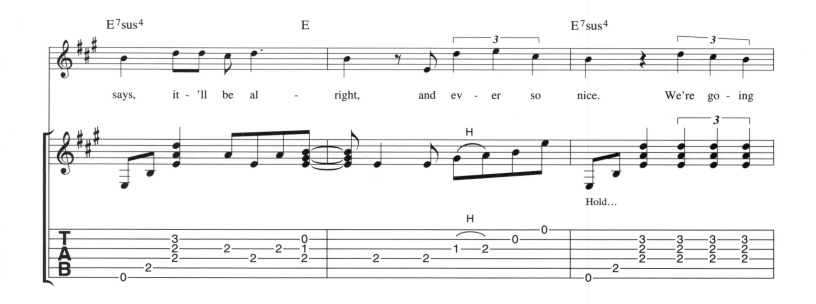

says, it-'ll be al - right, and ev - er so nice. We're go - ing

Hold…

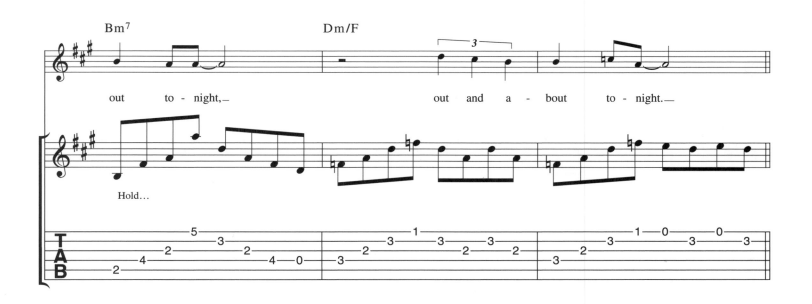

out to - night,— out and a - bout to - night.—

Hold…

𝄋 CHORUS

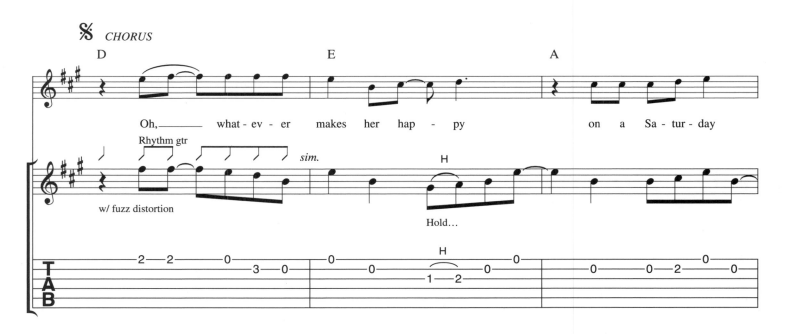

Oh,_____ what - ev - er makes her hap - py on a Sa - tur - day

Rhythm gtr   sim.

w/ fuzz distortion

Hold…

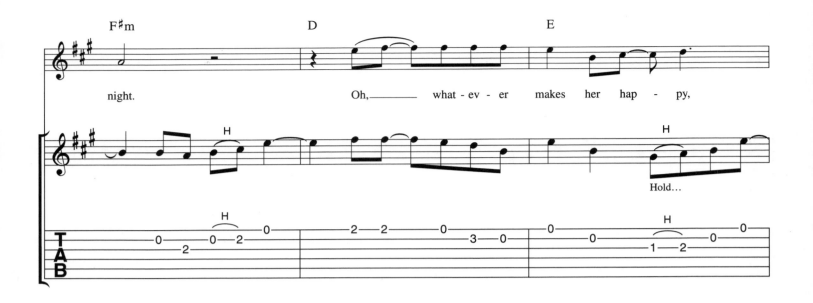

night.

Oh,_____ what - ev - er makes her hap - py,

Hold...

To Coda ⊕

1.   **2.**

what - ev - er makes it all right. _____ Ah._____ 2. To - Ah._____

Hold...

Gliss cancel fuzz   Gliss cancel fuzz

Gliss   Gliss

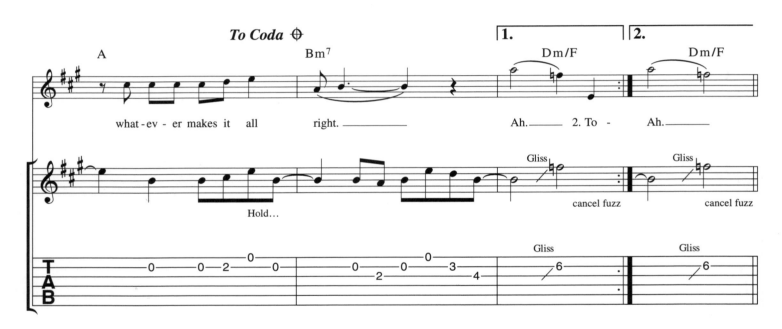

We'll go___ to freak shows___ and peep shows.___

Hold...   *sim.*

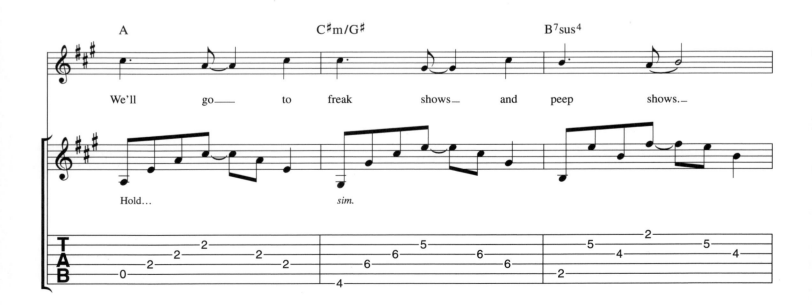

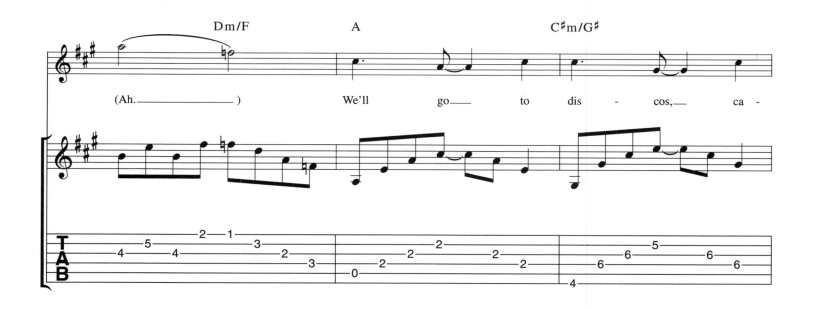

(Ah._____) We'll go___ to dis - cos,___ ca -

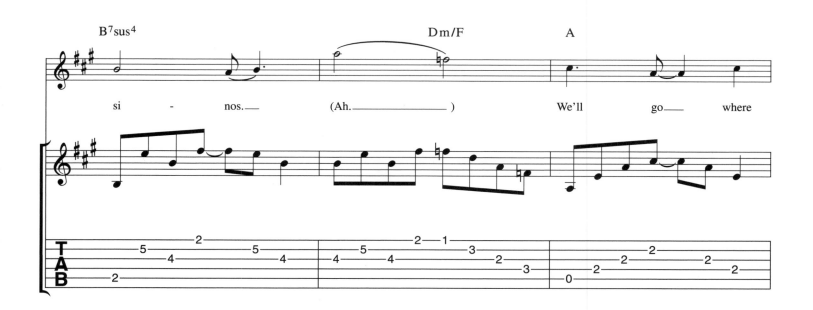

si - nos.___ (Ah._____) We'll go___ where

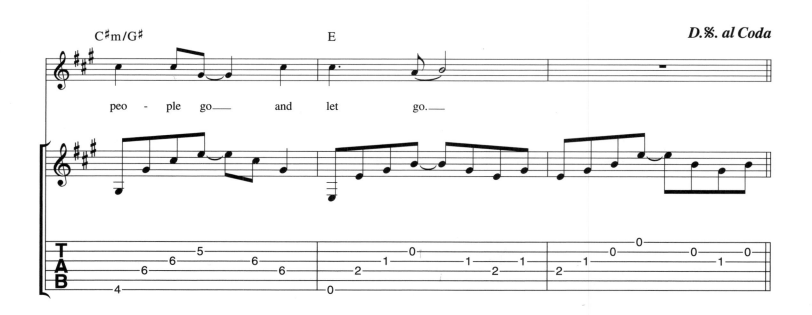

D.%. al Coda

peo - ple go___ and let go.___

⊕ Coda

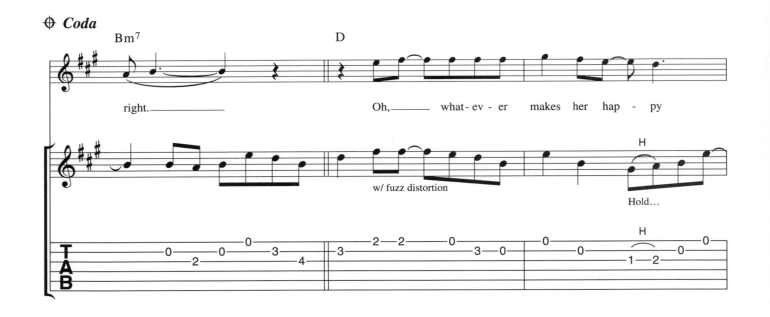

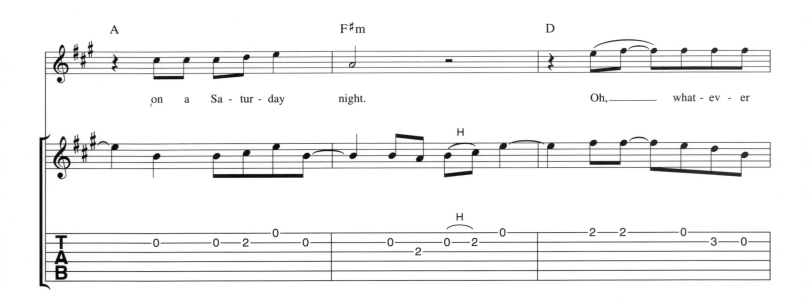

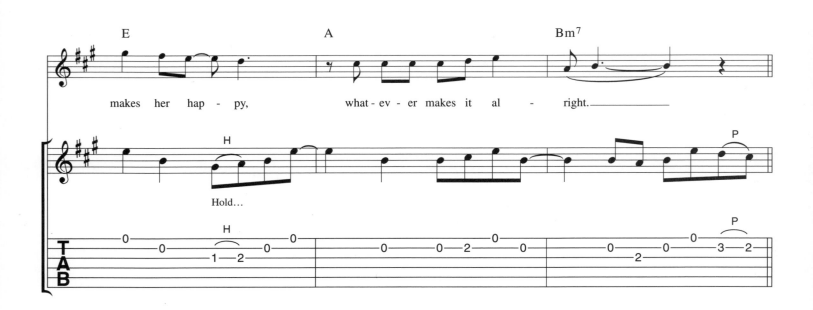

right.

Oh,_____ what-ev-er makes her hap-py

on a Sa-tur-day night.

Oh,_____ what-ev-er

makes her hap-py,

what-ev-er makes it al - right.

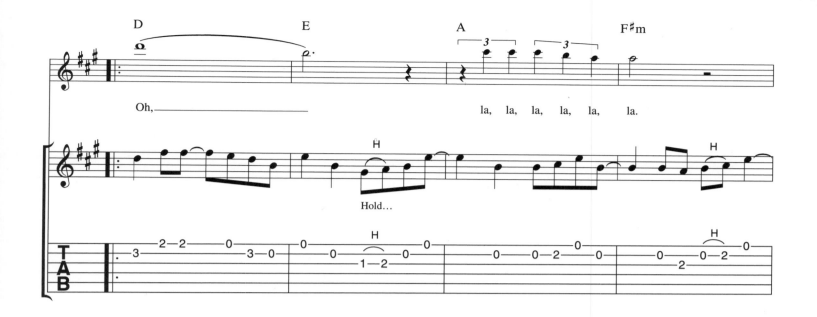

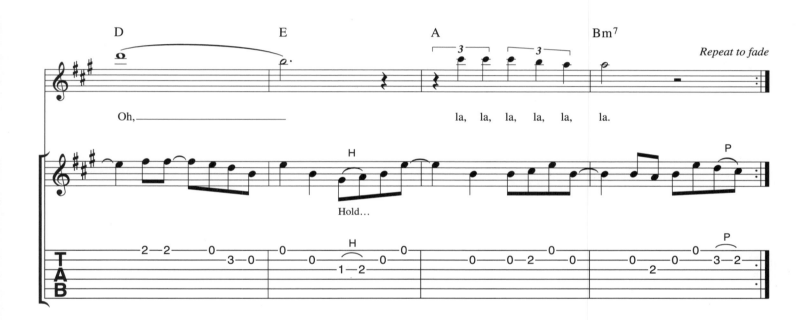

Verse 2:

Today she's been sat there, sat there in a black chair, office furniture
But it'll be alright
'Cos tonight we'll go drinking, we'll do silly things, and never let the winter in
And it'll be okay like everyone says, it'll be alright and ever so nice
We're going out tonight, out and about tonight.

Exclusive Distributors:
Music Sales Limited
8/9 Frith Street,London W1V 5TZ, England.
Music Sales Pty Limited
120 Rothschild Avenue Rosebery, NSW 2018,
Australia.

Order No.AM940940
ISBN 0-7119-6150-6

Music arranged by Arthur Dick.
Music processed by Paul Ewers Music Design.
Cover design by Peter Saville.
Text design by Michael Bell Design.

Printed in the United Kingdom by
Halstan & Co Ltd, Amersham, Buckinghamshire.

Your Guarantee of Quality:
As publishers, we strive to produce
every book to the highest commercial standards.
The music has been freshly engraved and,
whilst endeavouring to retain the original running
order of the recorded album, the book has been
carefully designed to minimise awkward page turns
and to make playing from it a real pleasure.
Particular care has been given to specifying acid-free,
neutral-sized paper made from pulps which have
not been elemental chlorine bleached.
This pulp is from farmed sustainable forests and
was produced with special regard for the environment.
Throughout, the printing and binding have been
planned to ensure a sturdy, attractive publication
which should give years of enjoyment.
If your copy fails to meet our high standards,
please inform us and we will gladly replace it.

Music Sales' complete catalogue describes
thousands of titles and is available in full colour sections
by subject, direct from Music Sales Limited.
Please state your areas of interest and send a cheque/
postal order for £1.50 for postage to: Music Sales Limited,
Newmarket Road, Bury St. Edmunds, Suffolk IP33 3YB.